SCIENCE ON PATROL

In SPACE

**Louise and
Richard Spilsbury**

Gareth Stevens
PUBLISHING

Please visit our website, www.garethstevens.com.
For a free color catalog of all our high-quality books,
call toll free 1-800-542-2595 or fax 1-877-542-2596.

Cataloging-in-Publication Data

Names: Spilsbury, Louise.
Title: In space / Louise and Richard Spilsbury.
Description: New York : Gareth Stevens, 2017. | Series: Science on patrol | Includes index.
Identifiers: ISBN 9781482459722 (pbk.) | ISBN 9781482459746 (library bound) | ISBN 9781482459739 (6 pack)
Subjects: LCSH: Space colonies--Juvenile literature. | Astronautics--Juvenile literature. | Outer space--Exploration--
  Juvenile literature.
Classification: LCC TL795.7 S65 2017 | DDC 629.4--dc23

First Edition

Published in 2017 by
Gareth Stevens Publishing
111 East 14th Street, Suite 349
New York, NY 10003

Copyright © 2017 Gareth Stevens Publishing

Produced for Gareth Stevens by Calcium
Editors: Sarah Eason and Jennifer Sanderson
Designers: Paul Myerscough and Simon Borrough
Picture researcher: Rachel Blount

Picture credits: Cover: Shutterstock: Andrey Armyagov (b), Kim Briers (tr), Alex Mit (tl); Inside: NASA: 6–7b, 14,
16, 18–19, 20, 23, 27, 30, 31, SpaceX 28–29t; Shutterstock: 3Dsculptor 15, Andrey Popov 41, BlueRingMedia
5, Andrea Danti 44–45, Ericsmandes 40, Jorg Hackemann 17, Marcel Clemens 12, Science photo 43, Somchai
Som 10–11, Johan Swanepoel 7, Triff 4, Vchal 11; Wikimedia Commons: NASA 1, 8, 9, 21, 22, 24, 32–33, 33b,
34, NASA/Crew of Expedition 8 25, NASA, ESA and the Hubble SM4 ERO Team 38, NASA/JPL 13, 42, NASA/
JPL-Caltech/Malin Space Science Systems 37, NASA/JPL-Caltech/Space Science Institute 35, NASA/MSFC/David
Higginbotham/Emmett Given 39, NASA/Kim Shiflett 3, 28.

Printed in China
CPSIA compliance information: Batch #CW17GS: For further information contact Gareth Stevens, New York, New York at 1-800-542-2595.

contents

CHAPTER 1

WORKING IN SPACE

Earth seems huge and important to us but it is actually a tiny rock in the vast expanse of space. Scientists who live and work in space have to cope with a highly challenging and dangerous environment. They explore the mysterious world beyond Earth's **atmosphere**: the stars, planets, and **galaxies** that make up the **universe**.

Where Is Space?

Outer space begins over 60 miles (100 kilometers) above the surface of Earth, where the atmosphere that surrounds our planet ends. It is where the blue sky we can see above Earth ends, and the blackness of space begins. Without air to scatter the sunlight and create the blue sky, outer space looks like a black nothingness dotted with stars. However, space is not completely empty. Gas, dust, pieces of rock, and other **matter** float around in **interstellar** space, and there are also planets and larger rocks called **asteroids**.

Space is a very challenging habitat in which to live and work.

Our Solar System

Mercury · Venus · Earth · Mars · Jupiter · Saturn · Uranus · Neptune

↑ The sun and the eight planets that orbit it together form the solar system.

Our Place in Space

Earth is one of eight planets that **orbit** the sun. Those planets and the sun form the galaxy known as the Milky Way—together with about 200 billion other stars, billions of other planets, and a collection of clouds of dust and gas. Almost everything we can see in the sky from Earth is part of the enormous Milky Way, although most of its stars are too far away for us to see them. The Milky Way is just one of billions more galaxies that together form the universe.

The Solar System

The sun is an ordinary star: a ball of constantly exploding superheated gases that release vast amounts of heat and light energy. The sun looks bigger and brighter than other stars because it is closer to Earth. The solar system is made up of the sun and the objects that move in orbit around it. Planets are giant, spherical objects that orbit a star. Earth is unusual among the eight planets in the solar system because it is just the right distance from the sun for life to exist here. It is neither too cold nor too hot, and it is the right temperature for water to exist in liquid form.

Challenges and Dangers

Space is full of challenges and dangers for scientists on patrol. As well as temperature extremes, space scientists, or astronauts, have to cope with a lack of air, **microgravity**, **radiation**, and fast-moving space junk.

Lack of Air

Beyond Earth's atmosphere, there is almost no air for humans to breathe, so scientists must take an air-supply system with them. Scientists outside a spacecraft and unprotected in space could survive for just a few minutes. They would not explode, as you sometimes see happening in movies. It is more likely that they would either die because their blood would boil, as a result of the decrease in **air pressure**, or they would quickly freeze to death because of the cold.

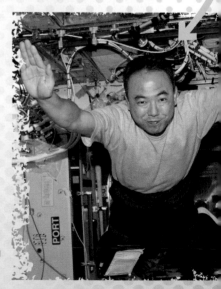

Scientists in a spacecraft in orbit look like they are floating!

Microgravity

One of the things people have to learn to get used to in space is microgravity. Gravity is a force of attraction that pulls two objects toward each other. It holds people on Earth's surface, keeps the moon in orbit around Earth, and Earth in orbit around the sun. Gravity becomes weaker the farther apart two objects are. A spacecraft in orbit is pulled by Earth's gravity and is falling toward Earth's surface, but because it moves so quickly, the curve of its fall matches the curve of Earth. Inside the spacecraft, scientists appear to be floating but they are actually falling toward Earth with their ship. That means they become **weightless**.

Radiation Danger

Some types of space radiation are dangerous to humans. They include the **infrared** and ultraviolet rays that come from the sun, and **cosmic rays** that come from distant galaxies. Cosmic rays are particles so tiny they cannot be seen, even with a microscope, but they move at the speed of light and are packed with energy. They can be harmful to people who are exposed to them for any length of time, possibly causing cancer and memory loss.

Space Junk

Space is full of rocks and pieces of discarded objects that were made on Earth, such as pieces left from rockets, tools dropped by scientists in space, or even flecks of paint from old spacecraft. This "junk," or debris, may not sound dangerous, but when it is moving at speeds of 17,500 miles per hour (28,164 kilometers per hour) it can cause a lot of damage if it hits something.

This is an illustration of space junk orbiting Earth.

SPACE LESSONS

Before scientists can go on patrol in space, they have to undergo years of training. As well as learning about the science of space and understanding how to conduct experiments or collect **samples** and **data** in space, they have to learn how to cope with the challenges of living beyond Earth's atmosphere.

Early Space Science

It took scientists many years to figure out how to put people into space safely. In 1942, a rocket reached space. Then, in 1947, the first animals—fruit flies—were launched into space. Scientists continued to study the effects of space on animals by sending a dog into space in 1957 and a monkey in 1959. The first humans went into space in 1961. By 1969, scientists were able to send the first astronauts to the moon. Since the 1980s, there have been many spacecraft carrying humans on missions into space.

Space scientists must train for microgravity on Earth. They may use a machine known as a vomit comet. As its name suggests, many of them are sick the first time they try it.

Space Skills

Astronauts learn how to deal with any problems that could happen in space, such as equipment failing to work, and how to deal with challenges such as microgravity. To get used to microgravity, they may train underwater in huge water tanks. They wear spacesuits and move in and around models of spacecraft.

In 1969, *Apollo 11* landed on the moon. Buzz Aldrin became one of the first two people ever to walk on its surface.

SCIENCE PATROL SURVIVAL

The moon has no liquid water, so the dust is like a fine powder that sticks to anything it touches. In 1972, the crew of *Apollo 17* forgot to brush the dust off their boots before reentering their spacecraft. The dust got into the air and caused sneezing, runny noses, and itchy eyes. The astronauts soon felt better, but this taught scientists that moon dust is made of tiny, rough, jagged grains, and it could do fatal damage to human lungs if a person breathed in too much of it.

How do you think the lessons learned by these early astronauts and scientists, and the discoveries they made, have helped the expeditions that have ventured into space since?

9

CHAPTER 2

Why Study Space?

Scientists study space to find out the answers to some important questions, such as how did our solar system form? How do galaxies form and change? Is there life or another habitable planet out there in the universe?

The Big Bang Theory

The Big Bang is the name for a theory space scientists have developed to explain how the universe formed. Almost 14 billion years ago, the entire universe was inside a hot, dense bubble that was thousands of times smaller than a pinhead. When this bubble exploded, it spread out from a single **atom** to the size of a galaxy. It cooled rapidly and tiny particles of matter formed. Some of these particles joined over time to form the stars and planets that make up the universe. The universe expanded very rapidly and it is still growing today.

The Origins of the Moon

Scientists think that the moon that orbits Earth was probably created when an object bumped into Earth when the planet was forming 4.5 billion years ago. The pieces of dust and rock that broke off in the impact eventually joined to form the moon. Scientists have figured this out because they have been able to collect samples of rock from the surface of the moon and discovered that these rocks are similar to those on Earth.

Black Holes

A black hole is a spot in space where matter has collapsed in on itself, so that there is a vast amount of mass in a tiny area. The gravitational pull of a black hole is so huge that nothing can escape—not even light. Scientists studying black holes cannot actually see them but know where they are because they affect dust, stars, and galaxies nearby.

Scientists detect black holes by the disks of material whirling around them that get very hot and release radiation.

studying PLANETS

Scientists learn a lot about the planets in our solar system from information they have collected while working on spacecraft and from unmanned missions into space.

The Eight Planets

The four planets closest to the sun are Mercury, Venus, Earth, and Mars. They have solid, rocky surfaces because the sun's heat burned off the gases inside them as they formed. Venus is the hottest planet, even though it is not closest to the sun, because it has a very thick atmosphere. Two of the outer planets—Jupiter and Saturn—are known as gas giants because they are massive balls of hydrogen and helium gases. Uranus and Neptune are farthest from the sun and are so cold and icy that they are called ice giants.

The gas giant planets have rings made from chunks of ice and rock, but none are as spectacular or as complicated as Saturn's.

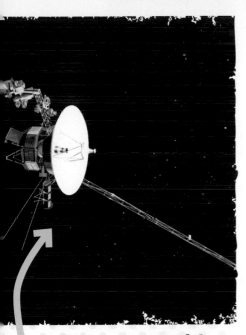

Scientists learned a lot about the ice and gas giant planets from images taken by the *Voyager* spacecraft, which flew past them.

Dwarf Planets

Until 2006, there were nine planets, including Pluto, in the solar system. This is when space scientists discovered there were many similar objects to Pluto. They decided to define a planet as an object in space that has a strong enough gravitational force to pull smaller, nearby objects toward it, leaving its own orbit clear. Large space objects without clear orbits, such as Pluto, are now called dwarf planets.

Asteroids and Meteoroids

There are other rocky objects in the solar system besides planets. Asteroids are large rocks up to 370 miles (600 kilometers) across, which orbit the sun. At least one new asteroid is discovered every year. Meteoroids are pieces of space rock that orbit the sun, too, but they can range in size from as tiny as dust particles to as big as a house. They usually burn up if they pass through Earth's atmosphere. If they survive and land on Earth they are called meteorites.

SCIENCE PATROL SURVIVAL

Scientists study planets to find out information such as what their atmospheres are like and if they could contain water or other useful **resources**. They also explore planets to find out if they could have been home to living things in the past.

As the world's population grows and people use up more of Earth's resources, how could this research help us? Explain your answer.

studying EARTH

Scientists also work from space to study Earth from a distance. From space they can learn vital information about the planet, its atmosphere, and how **global warming** is affecting it.

Earth Events

Scientists in space have a unique perspective on Earth. For example, they can take pictures every day to record Earth's surface changing over time, including events such as storms, floods, fires, and volcanic eruptions. The images they take can show where areas of **pollution** are, how much rainforest is being cut down, and how some cities are growing. These images help researchers on Earth understand the complex systems that make the planet work: how our planet and the different layers that make up its atmosphere work together in different ways to ensure our survival.

From space, scientists can see and take detailed images of the atmosphere around Earth and what is happening at its surface.

Space scientists also study how much pollution might be added to the atmosphere if space travel increases in the future, with new companies offering tourists the chance to visit space.

Global Warming

Climate is the average pattern of weather over a long time. Throughout history, the global climate has changed, sometimes getting hotter and at other times becoming much colder. The climate has been changing more rapidly in the last 150 years and scientists believe that, unlike climate change in the past, this is caused by human activities, such as burning **fossil fuels**. As people burn fossil fuels, we increase the amount of **greenhouse gases** in the atmosphere. Greenhouse gases trap some of the sun's heat that would otherwise reflect off Earth's surface and bounce back into space, so they help keep Earth at a comfortable temperature. However, as the quantity of greenhouse gases increases, Earth is becoming hotter—a phenomenon known as global warming.

Climate Models

Using detailed investigation of **satellite** observations as well as mathematical calculations about climate, called climate models, space scientists are exploring how and why human actions cause changes to the atmosphere and Earth's temperature. This helps them predict how fast these changes might happen. It also allows them to advise on the need to reduce the amount of greenhouse gases released into the air and limit the damage caused by global warming.

SPACE SURVIVAL

Space scientists do a lot of research on the effects of space on the human body, on other **organisms** such as plants, and on substances such as fire. This research could enable scientists to find ways to help humans to travel farther in space or even to live there safely.

The Effects of Microgravity

Space scientists at the National Aeronautics and Space Administration (NASA) research how microgravity in space affects metals, plants, the human body, and other things. On Earth, a person's body is constantly working against the force of gravity because the muscles and bones have to support his or her body weight all day long. In microgravity, astronauts experience weightlessness and the body does not need to work to support and move them, so their muscles and bones can become weaker. This can reduce their strength and ability to work. Space scientists study what microgravity does to astronauts so they can use this information to find ways to keep them safe and healthy. Scientists test how other things act differently in microgravity, too. For example, the roots of plants grow downward on Earth but not in space, and candle flames burn as blue circles in space because of different strengths of gravity.

Scientists grow plants in space to learn how to help them grow. They also test which plants are safe to eat when grown in space.

Radiation Research

Our planet's **magnetic field** protects people on Earth from almost all the harmful radiation that comes from the sun and deep space. Scientists are researching ways to keep astronauts and scientists safe from the sun's high radiation and cosmic rays in space, too. They are studying new materials to make better shields for blocking radiation and shields that could deflect dangerous space debris from spacecraft. The challenge is that such shields must be incredibly strong but also light. Lead would be an ideal metal for the job, but it is too heavy. Some scientists are also working on medical treatments to help people if they are exposed to solar or cosmic radiation.

Scientists research materials to make tiles like these on the *Explorer* spacecraft. The tiles act as a heat shield.

CHAPTER 3

LAB LiFe

There are telescopes that can see far into space, but to be able to research space in more depth, scientists need to be there. The International Space Station (ISS) is the ninth crewed space station. It is the third-brightest object in the sky, after the sun and moon. There, space scientists from around the world live and work in labs for weeks or months at a time, carrying out experiments inside and outside the ISS.

Building the ISS

Space stations are giant structures that are put into orbit around Earth. The ISS measures 240 feet (74 meters) long by 360 feet (110 meters) wide, which is slightly larger than a soccer pitch. As a result of its large size, it had to be constructed in space from parts that were delivered separately, piece by piece. There were (and are) no rockets big or powerful enough to carry the ISS into space in one piece.

In 1998, a Russian rocket carried the first piece of the ISS into space. Gradually, more pieces were added. By November 2000, the ISS was ready for the first crew to live on it, and there have been people living on it ever since. Scientists continued to add more parts to the ISS, and it was finally completed in 2011. As well as parts needed to assemble the ISS, many of the things that astronauts need to survive in space, such as air, food, and water, have also been transported to the ISS.

The ISS took 13 years to complete at an estimated cost of $100 billion. It is in orbit about 250 miles (400 kilometers) above Earth's surface.

SCIENCE PATROL SURVIVAL

The ISS is called the "International" Space Station because a partnership between European countries, the United States, Japan, Canada, and Russia built and manages it. Each country built a space module, or unit, of the ISS. Once these modules were joined in space, they formed the core of the ISS. The different countries who built the station use it together. It has labs run by the United States, Russia, Japan, and Europe. This allows countries around the world to carry out scientific research together and share their results.

Why do you think it is important to have international cooperation in space?

The Space Station

The ISS is built to withstand the challenges of space and to provide space scientists with everything they need to survive and work in orbit.

Station Parts

The modules where the scientists live and work are shaped like canisters and spheres. They are pressurized to hold the air that the scientists need to breathe, a little like the way soda is packaged in small canisters that hold the liquids inside under pressure, so they keep their bubbles. The modules are attached to the frame of the station, along with large, flat **solar panels** and radiators. Solar panels convert light energy from the sun into electrical energy. The radiators get rid of waste heat into the coldness of space so the ISS does not get too hot.

Spacecraft have standardized docking ports, so different types can attach to the ports on the ISS.

The solar panels on the ISS cover 27,000 square feet (2,500 square meters) and make enough electricity to power 10 average-sized homes.

Doors and Docking Ports

The ISS has sealed doors, called airlocks, which astronauts use to go outside the station without losing valuable air from inside. They may go on spacewalks, for example, to set up experiments on the outside of the ISS. Docking ports are larger doors that spacecraft connect to when they bring supplies, equipment, and visitors.

Water and Air

It would be impossible to transport enough water to the ISS from Earth because water is heavy. Instead, the ISS has water-recycling systems. Machines similar to air conditioners collect **water vapor** from air breathed out by scientists and crew, and steam from showers. These machines capture 53 pounds (24 kilograms) of water each day. In case of emergencies when the water recycling machines cannot work, there are reserve tanks of water. Other machines remove poisonous carbon dioxide from air breathed out by astronauts, and convert some of the water into oxygen to breathe. Visiting spacecraft also bring tanks of air to replenish supplies.

21

LIFE ON A SPACE STATION

Life for scientists working on the ISS is nothing like life on Earth. The ISS is traveling at speeds of 17,500 miles per hour (28,000 kilometers per hour), so it takes just 90 minutes for it to make a complete orbit of Earth. That means astronaut scientists working and living on the ISS see a sunrise or sunset every 45 minutes.

Daily Life

While living in space means scientists see great views, life on a space station has its challenges. For one thing, the place where the six members of the crew live and work for the majority of the time is only about the size of a school bus. Each astronaut has his or her own room, known as a galley, where they sleep. At bedtime, they have to strap themselves into their beds to keep from floating around. When they go to the bathroom, they have to strap themselves to a toilet that has a special device for sucking away waste.

The ISS kitchen has special microwave ovens in which astronauts can prepare some of the same foods they enjoy at home.

Dressed for Work

During daylight periods, temperatures outside the ISS reach 392° Fahrenheit (200° Celsius). Temperatures during the night drop to -328° Fahrenheit (-200° Celsius). However, inside the ISS, temperatures are kept at a constant 70° Fahrenheit (21° Celsius). That means that astronauts can wear the clothing they would usually wear at home. They change into clumsy spacesuits only when they go outside the station on spacewalks.

Space Gyms

When people use a treadmill on the ISS, they have to be tied onto it with harnesses that pull them down to the walking surface.

There is also a gym on the ISS where astronauts exercise for at least two hours every day. Exercise is very important, because microgravity affects bones and muscles in space. If astronauts do not exercise, they will lose bone and muscle mass. They use special exercise equipment to make sure they do not lose too much bone or muscle mass, which would be dangerous for them once they return to Earth. They use a variety of exercise machines.

Inside the Lab

Scientific research on the ISS takes place in the six labs. Different space agencies from Europe and countries such as the United States, Russia, and Japan own and run each lab. Like many labs on Earth, each lab is crammed with equipment to do a variety of experiments, with the difference being the space lab kit is very compact because it all had to be carried up there from Earth.

Destiny Laboratory

The U.S. Destiny laboratory is a 28-foot (8.5 meter) long box with a very clear window at the end. This enables scientists to have exceptional views and take photographs of Earth. All four walls are lined with racks to hold modules. The racks have fluid and electrical connectors to the modules, **sensors**, and digital video cameras to view and record experiments, and stream data to Earth. Different space missions have different experiments to carry out, so modules are replaced and exchanged. The modules include the Microgravity Space Glovebox (MSG) and WetLab-2.

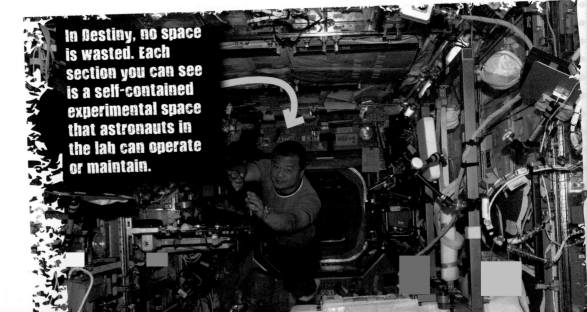

In Destiny, no space is wasted. Each section you can see is a self-contained experimental space that astronauts in the lab can operate or maintain.

The MSG is a special sealed unit that space scientists can use to carry out experiments safely. It ensures no substances escape accidentally.

The MSG

The MSG is around twice the size of an airline carry-on bag, with a large front window. Scientists carry out experiments in microgravity conditions in the MSG. They can handle dangerous substances using rugged, sealed gloves attached to holes on the sides of the MSG. A video system and data downlinks allow the enclosed experiments to be controlled from Earth, too.

WetLab-2

WetLab-2 is a compact device that detects how the **genes** in living **cells** are working at different times, based on the chemicals they produce. The sealed unit analyzes the chemicals without letting them escape. It is useful for noticing how being in space changes the health, growth, or stress levels of living things, from **bacteria** to the astronauts themselves.

CHAPTER 4

Out and About

To travel into space and to explore it while they are there, scientists on patrol use a variety of machines and equipment. Rockets are powerful vehicles that fly from Earth to space. They are used to launch satellites, **probes**, and spacecraft into space.

Rockets

Rockets need a lot of force to escape Earth's gravity. Rocket engines use solid or liquid fuel, or a combination of both. In a combustion chamber, they turn these fuels into very hot gases. The engine pushes the gases out of its back through an exhaust nozzle. As the gases are pushed out of the back of the rocket, they create a **thrust** force that pushes the rocket upward or forward. Many rockets have a main engine and extra, smaller booster rockets attached to their side. These give the rocket an extra push for takeoff. After the boosters have used up all their fuel, they drop off and fall into the ocean.

G-Forces

We do not notice the force of gravity on Earth, but as a rocket shoots upward through Earth's atmosphere, people inside the spacecraft experience 3 G-forces. These are gravitational forces three times higher than normal. They feel like they are being pushed back into their seats, so their bodies feel heavy and it is hard for them to move their arms. The body's fluids weigh more, so the heart pumps faster to circulate the blood. This could make people dizzy or pass out, so astronauts have to wear special suits and train to cope with G-forces before takeoff.

Flying in Orbit

Once a rocket travels beyond the atmosphere, there is no air. This means there is no **air resistance** to slow rockets down. They can keep moving fast without needing to burn fuel. They need to turn on the engines and burn fuel only to change direction or to speed up. Astronauts fire up the engines to get themselves out of orbit and on course to where they want to go, then they can turn them off and coast along.

Gases shooting out of the engine at high speed push a rocket upward.

REUSABLE SPACECRAFT

Most rockets fly only once. That is because they need to use all of their available fuel in order to get their **payload** into space. Other spacecraft are designed to be used again and again.

Space Shuttles

Space shuttles were the world's first reusable spacecraft. They were used from 1981 to 2011 to transport scientists, crews, and supplies to and from the ISS. Space shuttles blasted off with the help of rockets, but were flown back to Earth like an airplane, dropping wheels from their underside and rolling to a stop on a runway. Although the space shuttle was technically reusable, as it took off, it discarded its solid fuel boosters, which were then retrieved from the ocean. It also dumped its huge fuel tank, which burned up in the atmosphere. These things were expensive to replace and refurbish. Since 2011, the *Soyuz* Russian spacecraft has carried most people and supplies to and from the ISS.

The space shuttle was 184 feet (56 meters) tall with an orbiter that housed the passengers. This was 122 feet (37 meters) long.

Discovery

United States

New Spaceships

Private companies are testing new reusable spacecraft that will be used to carry people and cargo to the ISS and into orbit. The 30-foot-long (9 meter) winged *Dream Chaser* is like a small space shuttle and is much more compact than the original shuttles. It is designed to carry up to seven astronauts into low-Earth orbit. Another spacecraft is the SpaceX *Dragon V2*, which is shaped more like a rocket. The first *Dragon* has been carrying cargo to and from the ISS since 2012, but *Dragon V2* has a pressurized section, or capsule, that can carry both cargo and people into space.

Dragon V2 is 23.6 feet (7.2 meters) tall and has seats for seven passengers.

SCIENCE PATROL SURVIVAL

Rockets usually discard their fuel tank after takeoff and then, as a result of the **friction** with the atmosphere, the heat-shield casing burns away to protect the capsule with the crew inside. Only the capsule survives. This process has been compared to building a 747 airplane and flying it only once, empty, before the pilot bails out near the destination in a small capsule attached to the front of the jet, while the jet burns away to nothing.

Why do you think it is important to develop reusable spacecraft? Why might this mean there may be more spaceships in the future?

When space scientists go outside the space station on a spacewalk, for example, to set up science experiments, they wear spacesuits to survive the dangers of space. They also need to carry an oxygen supply so they can breathe.

Spacesuits

Spacesuits have a strong outer layer to protect the wearer from pieces of orbiting space dust that move faster than bullets and could injure them. The suits also protect astronauts from the extremes of heat and cold in space and keep them at a comfortable temperature. They have layers of **insulation** and can pump warm or cool fluid through pipes inside the suit. A backpack supplies scientists with the oxygen they need to breathe and lasts for about seven hours. The low air pressure in space would make people swell up and damage their bodies, so there is a fan in the backpack that moves air around the suit. This keeps the air pressure inside the suit the same as it would be for people on Earth. That is why a spacesuit looks puffed-up.

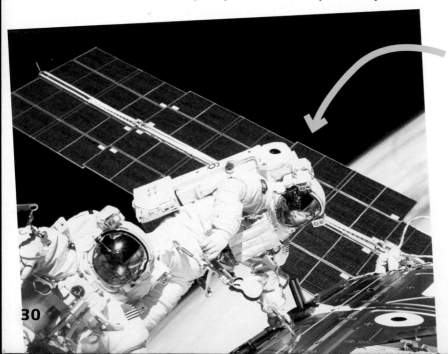

Spacesuits not only supply oxygen for people to breathe when they are on a spacewalk, but also water for them to drink.

If an astronaut became separated from the space station, he or she could use a jetpack to fly back.

Spacewalks

Space scientists never really walk on a spacewalk. In microgravity, people hover or float, so they have to be attached to the ISS by strong safety cords to keep them from floating away. They also have to clip tools and equipment to their spacesuits to keep them from drifting away. Some spacewalks are made using a **robotic arm** to move the astronaut into position. The ISS has handrails on the outside that astronauts can use to pull themselves around the craft. Spacewalks can last for several hours.

Jetpacks

Some scientists wear a type of jetpack when they are outside the ISS. This could save them in case of an emergency in which they become detached from their safety cords. The jetpack has small thruster jets that can be pointed in different directions to help the astronaut move around and get back to safety.

CHAPTER 5

CUTTING-EDGE TECHNOLOGY

Some of the most high-tech machines ever invented are at work in space. Many of these are robots, which are machines capable of carrying out a complex series of actions automatically, usually programmed by remote control or by a computer.

Robotic Arms

A robotic arm is made up of several parts, a little like a human arm. The end of a robot arm can carry a variety of objects, from grippers to pick up or hold things to tools such as drills or wrenches. On space stations, robotic arms carry out all sorts of jobs on the exterior, such as constructing new parts of the station itself. Canadarm 2 is the biggest robotic arm in space, and it is strong enough to lift more than 110 tons (100 tonnes), yet delicate enough to grip bolts that are only 1 inch (2.5 centimeters) across. It attaches to electrical supply ports dotted around the space station and can shift from one to another, a little like a looping caterpillar.

Flying Robots

SPHERES are small flying robots that look like soccer balls. They move around the ISS using small thrusters, forcing out carbon dioxide into the ISS atmosphere. SPHERES avoid crashing into objects using sensors, which are similar to parking sensors on automobiles, and by varying their thrust directions. They navigate by sensing their distance from **beacons** in fixed positions around the ship.

Robonaut

The most lifelike robot in space is called Robonaut. It has long arms and a head with several cameras behind its visor. These feed images to a controller's screen or detect its distance from objects. Robonaut can be programmed to carry out routine tasks, such as cleaning surfaces. It can even move around on gripping, flexible legs, which have feet that can sense where the robot is going.

Scientists can be attached to Canadarm 2 to move safely around the ISS.

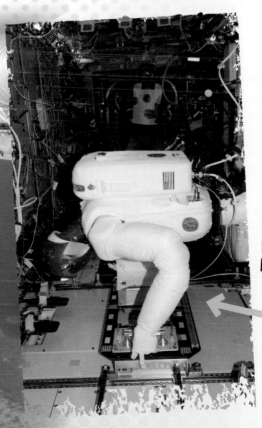

Robonaut can be operated by a person wearing virtual-reality equipment. Goggles in the helmet can see what the robot sees through its cameras. Tilting the helmet or flexing the glove makes Robonaut's head and hands move, too.

probes and ORBITERS

The farthest that astronauts have traveled in space has been the moon. However, cutting-edge robotic technology has allowed us to learn a lot about the other objects in our solar system.

Space Probes

A space probe is a robot spacecraft that collects scientific information by getting nearer to planets, moons, **comets**, and asteroids. Some probes even reach the surfaces of other planets. Probes traveling far from the sun are in near darkness, so solar panels cannot work to power them. Instead, they contain devices that convert the heat produced from the natural decay of **nuclear fuel** into electricity. This is used to operate cameras to take images and footage, devices called magnetometers for measuring magnetic forces produced by planets, and sensors that can measure the heat from objects as well as detect their movements. Probes carry large antennae dishes and aerials to send information automatically to Earth via radio signals. Most probes are on a very long, one-way trip, but will keep sending information for as long as their power lasts.

Probes carry delicate instruments inside that need to be tough enough to work for years, even when traveling in the extreme temperatures of space and at very fast speeds.

This incredible picture is made up from many pictures taken by the *Cassini* orbiter when it was 3.9 million miles (6.3 million kilometers) from Saturn and its rings.

Orbiters

Orbiters are built to fly in orbit around a planet and collect information about it over a long period of time, rather than just passing by like a probe. Spacecraft would normally be pulled toward a planet when they get close to it, because of the planet's gravitational pull. However, orbiters stay the same height above the surface of a planet by flying on a very fast circular path around it. Orbiters can be small robots but some, such as *Cassini*, are the size of a school bus. *Cassini*'s instruments include radar to map the changing cloud patterns around Saturn, which are evidence of its wind speeds, and cameras that have detected new rings around the planet.

LANDERS and ROVERS

Although scientists can learn a lot about planets from orbiting spacecraft, detailed observations must be made on a planet's surface. A lander is an unmanned spacecraft that lands on the surface of a planet to take images. It can also deliver **rovers** there. Landers do not move around once they have landed, but rovers can move around to study a planet's surface and collect samples.

Sky Crane

The sky crane is a robotic lander that was developed to lower a rover called Curiosity onto the surface of Mars. The sky crane looks a little like a huge jetpack and has eight thrusters. As it descended to the surface of Mars in 2012, heat shields protected it from the intense heat created by friction with the Martian atmosphere. This friction, along with a 60-foot-wide (18 meter) parachute, slowed the sky crane's descent. Near the surface, the parachute was detached, and the sky crane fired its thrusters in order to slow its descent so that it could lower Curiosity gently down onto the surface of Mars. Then, the bolts holding the rover to the lander exploded, separating the two. The sky crane drifted away from Curiosity and crashed into the surface, where it was destroyed.

Curiosity has six wide wheels and a suspension system that allows it to roll over rocks or other obstacles and to travel an average speed of 98 feet per hour (30 meters per hour).

The Curiosity Rover

Rovers are designed to look for and locate interesting rocks and soils and then to move to those areas and study them. The Curiosity rover is about 9 feet (2.8 meters) long and weighs about 2,000 pounds (900 kilograms). Scientists based on Earth operate it and it has equipment on board that makes it like a mobile science laboratory. It has a robotic arm 7 feet (2.1 meters) long that can hold and use several tools and instruments. These can collect samples of rock and analyze the chemicals that make up rocks and soils. Cameras take closeup and very detailed images of the surface of Mars.

SPACE TELESCOPES

Space scientists working on Earth use high-tech telescopes to view stars, planets, and distant galaxies. Telescopes are devices that can collect many times more light than the human eye, helping people see objects far away.

This amazing image of a faraway star, one of the hottest known stars in our galaxy, was taken by the Hubble Space Telescope.

The Hubble Space Telescope

There are powerful telescopes on Earth, but the clouds and atmosphere make it difficult for scientists to see details in space. The Hubble Space Telescope was launched into space in 1990. In space, there is very little gas and dust to blur the view of distant objects. Hubble has a digital camera that has taken many color pictures of distant stars, planets, and galaxies. It sends the images to scientists on Earth to help them learn more about the universe.

The mirrors on the James Webb Space Telescope are covered in a very thin layer of gold. This makes them excellent at reflecting infrared light. Each mirror is about the size of a coffee table, and behind each one are motors that can focus the telescope out in space.

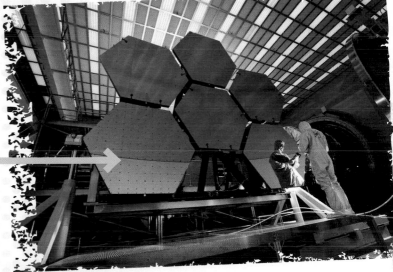

The James Webb Space Telescope

The James Webb Space Telescope is named after the person who was the head of NASA in the 1960s. This is the most powerful telescope ever built and is seven times bigger than Hubble. It consists of 18 mirror segments that fold up inside the rocket for launch. When the mirrors open in space, they work as one, making the telescope as wide as a tennis court and as tall as a three-story building. Once it launches, the James Webb Space Telescope will be placed 1 million miles (1.6 million kilometers) from Earth, nearly four times as far as the distance from Earth to the moon. The telescope will study the history of the universe and the formation of solar systems that might be capable of supporting life on planets similar to Earth. It also has a sun shield to protect it from the light and heat of the sun, Earth, and moon.

CHAPTER 6

Amazing Discoveries

As well as remarkable discoveries about black holes, stars, the planets, and other objects in space, some of the discoveries space scientists have made have had a huge impact on Earth.

Medical Advances

Scientists' research into keeping astronauts healthy in space aids people on Earth. Technology devised for space shuttle fuel pumps has been adapted to develop an artificial heart that can help people with heart disease. NASA technology has created an instrument for hospitals that analyzes blood in 30 seconds—previously it took 20 minutes. The light, hard material developed to protect space shuttle fuel tanks is being used to make better false limbs.

Technology developed by space scientists has made false limbs stronger, better, and cheaper.

Safety First

Foam insulation developed to protect the *Apollo* spacecraft is now used on oil pipelines, where temperature control is vital. Firefighters now use lightweight breathing systems and fire-resistant textiles designed for space. Sensitive cameras used to detect rays in space can also be used to spot forest fires. **Global Positioning System (GPS)** software that helps spacecraft determine their position is being used by airplane pilots to find their position to within 3 feet (1 meter). Scientists also developed systems to clean petroleum-based pollutants from water.

Useful Gadgets and Materials

Spacecraft and other space equipment are crammed with new technology useful on Earth. NASA developed the process for freeze-drying foods for the *Apollo* missions in the 1960s. Scientists working on microgravity experiments developed larger and better quality silicon chips to help them. These are now used in computers and many other electronic machines on Earth. One-third of all cell phone cameras use technology originally developed for NASA spacecraft. Cordless drills and computer joysticks were both developed for space missions. The technology used to make space boots has been adapted to make the cushioned soles in sneakers.

Coatings scientists developed for space helmet visors are used to make the lenses in glasses, sunglasses, and ski goggles 10 times more scratch resistant.

MISSION TO MARS

The discoveries space scientists are making are helping them find ways to allow people to travel deeper into space than ever before. There are already plans to send a mission to Mars.

Life on Mars

Scientists have been studying Mars for a long time. They have figured out that, of all the planets, it is the one that most resembles Earth. Like Earth, Mars has a solid, rocky surface. It has seasons and days as long as those on our planet. Scientists know that Mars is a cold planet with an ice cap at its South Pole. They hope that if people live there, they will be able to melt ice to make water to drink.

Some scientists believe that in the distant future people may be able to live on other planets such as Mars.

Thin Atmosphere

One problem with Mars is that its atmosphere is very thin and consists mostly of carbon dioxide. Scientists are researching how to build sealed structures that people could safely live in on Mars. They are investigating ways to covert the carbon dioxide in the atmosphere into oxygen that people can breathe. One way to do this is to grow plants on Mars. Plants use energy from the sun to turn carbon dioxide into oxygen during the process of photosynthesis, by which they make food.

Getting to Mars

Mars is at least 34.8 million miles (56 million kilometers) away from Earth, so scientists are researching the possibility of using a gravity assist maneuver to get a spacecraft carrying people there. Gravity assist allows spacecraft to use different paths or orbit to help them move between planets. The idea is that a spacecraft orbiting Earth would suddenly switch on its engines and speed up in order to leave Earth's orbit at a particular moment. The planet's gravity would give the spacecraft more energy and fling it farther into space, like a slingshot. The timing and speed of this maneuver would have to be carefully figured out so the spacecraft could meet up with Mars on that planet's own orbital path.

Biosphere 2 was a huge, sealed glasshouse built in the Arizona desert as an experiment in Mars survival.

patrolling the future

In the future, it could be even more important for science patrols to carry out research in space. Who knows, as Earth's population increases and the planet's resources become even more stretched, will we look to other planets for places to live or resources we can use?

Space Futures

There are many ideas about how scientists might study and explore space in the future. One idea of how to send people on long missions in the future is by freezing them first, to keep them alive but resting on very long journeys. They would then wake at their distant destination. Another is to send families on very, very long voyages so that later generations would reach their destination. These ideas may seem fanciful now, but remember that is what people thought about humans walking on the moon before 1969!

Future Labs

The ISS is expected to operate until 2024, so scientists are already busy planning ideas for new space stations. One idea is for a space station shaped like a giant mushroom. The long part would be a cylinder that would rotate four times per minute to create artificial gravity inside the station, so scientists would not feel weightless and could walk around normally, as they would on Earth. The Bigelow Expandable Activity Module (BEAM) is an expandable habitat that is already being tested on the ISS. These inflatable modules are light and small enough to transport on a rocket, but expand in space to potentially provide a comfortable area for scientists to live and work.

People have some amazing ideas of what space stations could look like in the future.

SCIENCE PATROL SURVIVAL

Working in space is challenging, difficult, and sometimes even dangerous. Scientists need somewhere to work productively and live and relax comfortably. Imagine you are going to design your own space station. What will you include there?

- *What will your space station look like?*
- *Will your station consist of several modules or only one?*
- *How many labs will you include and what will they be used to study?*
- *How will the station be powered?*

Glossary

air pressure a push of air on the surface of objects

air resistance the force of air that slows down a car or an airplane

asteroids large chunks of rock in the solar system

atmosphere the blanket of gases around a planet

atom the smallest unit of an element

bacteria tiny living things

beacons devices that can send out radio signals (or light)

cells the basic building blocks of all living things except viruses

comets objects in space made of ice, water, dust, and gases

cosmic rays energy-packed particles in space

data facts and statistics

fossil fuels fuels such as oil or natural gas, formed from plants and animals that died millions of years ago

friction the pushing force that slows down objects when they slide against each other

galaxies huge systems of stars, dust, and gases held together by gravity

genes instructions inside the cells of living things that determine what they are and look like

Global Positioning System (GPS) a system that uses signals from satellites in space to locate positions on Earth

global warming changes in the world's weather patterns caused by human activity

greenhouse gases gases that trap heat in the atmosphere

infrared a type of light that is invisible

insulation material that keeps heat or cold from passing through it

interstellar the space between the stars

magnetic field the invisible area of magnetic force around an object such as Earth

matter something that occupies space, has mass, and can exist as a solid, liquid, or gas

microgravity very weak gravity that creates a feeling of weightlessness in astronauts

nuclear fuel fuel such as uranium that is used in nuclear reactors as a source of electricity

orbit the path one object in space takes around another

orbiter an unmanned spacecraft that flies in orbit around a planet to collect images and data for a long time

organisms living things

payload cargo carried to space on a rocket

pollution something that adds dirty, harmful, or dangerous substances to air, water, soil, or space

probes unmanned spacecraft used to explore and record space

radiation energy in the form of waves or particles

resources things that people need or use such as oil and freshwater

robotic arm a device operated by people, for grabbing and lifting heavy things

rovers machines that move around on a planet's surface to collect images and samples

samples representative parts or single items from a larger whole or group

satellite electronic devices high in space that move around Earth

sensors devices that detect and measure something such as amounts of a particular gas in the air

solar panels panels designed to absorb the sun's energy and use it to make electricity

thrust a force usually produced by an engine to push a vehicle forward

universe everything that exists including all space and objects in it

water vapor when water is a gas in the air. Water comes in three states: ice (solid), water (liquid), and water vapor (gas).

weightless having no pull of gravity on a mass

For more information

Books

Carney, Elizabeth. *Mars: The Red Planet.* Washington, DC: National Geographic Children's Books, 2016.

Englert, Christoph. *Destination: Space.* New York, NY: Wide Eyed Editions, 2016.

Solar System (Collins Fascinating Facts). New York, NY: HarperCollins, 2016.

Space Visual Encyclopedia. New York, NY: Dorling Kindersley, 2016.

Websites

Watch as the ISS is built in this NASA animation of its decade-long assembly at:
www.space.com/10115-building-international-space-station.html

Visit NASA's Space Place for facts, videos and animations, space games, and activities at:
www.spaceplace.nasa.gov

Find out more about space and learn fascinating facts at:
www.dkfindout.com/uk/space

index